Foreword by Martin Bell

I am delighted to be asked to write the forev [illegible] and other Winter Sports. I am privileged enou [illegible] downhill skiing, but you do not have to be an [illegible] of pleasure from watching or taking part in winte [illegible] s.

For all athletes and sports fans the 1988 season has that special "feel" about it that comes with it being an Olympic year. The Olympics provide two weeks of exciting winter sports action every four years, but the sports are there to be enjoyed every year. In this book you can find out what is involved in many popular winter sports, Olympic and non-Olympic.

The 1988 Winter Olympics are being held in Calgary, Canada, and I will be there with the rest of the British team. To many athletes, the Olympics are more important than any other competition they enter. For ski-racers such as myself, everything is decided in one race, in the space of less than two minutes, and success can mean glory for many years to come. I had my first taste of the Olympics in 1984 at Sarajevo, Yugoslavia. Like most first-timers I was overawed by the security arrangements at first, but you soon realize that you are facing the same competitors as usual and that you had better concentrate on the race to come. The men's downhill was delayed for a week due to bad weather and I spent my fair share of the time in the free video games arcade in the Olympic Village. But I also managed to watch some Olympic ice-hockey, which was very exciting. It made me think how different team sports are to individual events, and how frustrating I would find it to have to rely on team-mates for a chance of winning a medal.

When at last we started racing, nerves affected my practice runs and the best position I could manage was 28th, but on the day, even with the 'flu, I came 18th, a great improvement. I am looking for an even better performance in Calgary and, although no Briton has yet won a medal in a skiing event, I will be giving 100% to try and change that record.

Martin Bell

Winter Sports and the Olympic Winter Games

There is a wide variety of winter sports, from the many different skiing events to speed and figure skating, bobsleigh and luge racing and team sports such as ice-hockey and curling. All of these are becoming increasingly popular with spectators as well as participants and you can find out about each of them later in this book.

Each sport holds its own international competitions and championships but probably the best occasion to see the top competitors in many of the sports is during the Olympic Winter Games, which you can read about below.

How the Games began

The modern Olympic Games began in 1896, but separate Winter Olympics did not exist until 1924. On this page there is a brief history of how the Winter Olympics evolved from the Summer competition.

The Olympic movement started at the end of the 19th Century. It was headed by a Frenchman, Baron Pierre de Coubertin, who dreamed of reviving the kind of sports festivals held in Ancient Greece. One of the most famous of these was the Olympic Games, held at Olympia every four years for 1000 years up to AD393.

According to Coubertin's ideals, the new Games should include as many popular sports as possible (meaning those that were widely practised in many countries), should promote healthy, sporting competition and encourage world peace through a great international event. All athletes taking part were to be amateurs, that is, not earning money from their sport and the contests were to be between individuals and teams, not countries. The first modern Olympic Games were held in the summer of 1896 in Athens.

The Olympic Winter Games

It was never part of Coubertin's plan to have a separate Winter Games. He did not consider that most winter sports were popular enough to qualify as Olympic, anyway. Exceptions were figure skating and ice-hockey, which were enjoyed by many people and were able to be included in Olympic Summer competitions on artificial ice-rinks. Figure skating has therefore featured in the Olympics since 1908, and ice-hockey since 1920.

Figure skaters wore long skirts and knee-breeches in 1908.

When the Games first began, skiing was most popular in the Scandinavian countries. They held their own international competitions in cross-country, biathlon and ski jumping (called Nordic events) and most of them did not see any need for an Olympic competition, so calls from some athletes for a Winter event were unsuccessful.

Skiing became more widespread, however, as downhill and slalom skiing (called alpine skiing) were pioneered in Switzerland and Austria during the early years of the 20th Century. Tobogganing and bobsleigh, which had been practised for years, became well-organized (The International Federation of Bobsleigh and Tobogganing was formed in 1923) and calls for an independent Winter Olympics grew.

One style of tobogganing in the 1890s.

These are early downhill skiers.

The International Olympic Committee (IOC), who organized the Games, resisted a Winter event for a long time but, in 1924, gave its support to an International Sports Week, held in Chamonix, Switzerland, featuring Winter Sports. Two years later, those in favour of Winter Olympics managed to change the minds of the IOC. The Chamonix Sports Week was retrospectively called the First Winter Games and Olympic Winter Games have been held every four years since, except during World War II (1939-1945).

Sports in the Winter Olympics

The first few Winter Games featured events in Nordic skiing, figure and speed skating, ice-hockey and bobsleigh. Despite the popularity of alpine skiing, events in this sport were not included until 1936. The luge was first competed in its present form (see page 22) in 1964, when it replaced different-style toboggan events such as the Cresta Run (see page 22).

New events are being introduced all the time, such as women's speed skating (1960), the 90 metre ski-jump (1964) and ice dance (1976).

Curling is a demonstration sport (see below) in the 1988 Games.

All the events to be included in an Olympics are decided by the IOC six years beforehand. In any Olympics there may be up to three demonstration events. These are events which the participants would like to have accepted into the Olympic programme. To succeed, the sport must prove itself to be widely practised in 25 countries over three continents, according to the present rules.

Governing bodies

The International Olympic Committee (IOC) is in charge of the organization and development of the Olympic Games. All countries involved in the Olympic Movement have representatives on the Committee. Most countries have only one representative, but some, such as those that have previously hosted the Games, are allowed two. At present there are 92 IOC members.

Regulations and safety standards in the Winter Olympics are controlled by International Federations, such as the Federation Internationale de Ski (F.I.S), formed in 1924 to control skiing competitions, and the International Skating Union (ISU) which controls speed and figure skating.

Winter Olympics venues

This is a list of all the Winter Olympics venues up to 1992. It was originally intended that the same country should hold the Summer and Winter Games but this proved impractical, since few countries could provide the facilities and weather conditions for both events. Only the U.S.A in 1932 and Germany in 1936 managed to do so.

1924 Chamonix, France. Retrospectively called the First Winter Games in 1926.

1928 St. Moritz, Switzerland. Unprecedented warm weather disrupted these Games.

1932 Lake Placid, U.S.A. Snow had to be imported from Canada this year.

1936 Garmisch-Partenkirchen, Germany. Alpine events included for the first time.

1940 and 1944 World War II. No Olympic Games.

1948 St. Moritz, Switzerland. Germany and Japan did not compete.

1952 Oslo, Norway. First capital city to hold an Olympics.

1956 Cortina d'Ampezzo, Italy. First Winter Olympics to be televised.

1960 Squaw Valley, U.S.A. First purpose-built resort for the Games.

1964 Innsbruck, Austria. Computers used for scoring for the first time.

1968 Grenoble, France. East and West Germany competed separately for the first time.

1972 Sapporo, Japan. First Games to be held outside Western Europe or the USA.

1976 Innsbruck, Austria. Used the same facilities as in 1964.

1980 Lake Placid, U.S.A. First to win five golds in one Games was Eric Heiden (USA), in speed skating.

1984 Sarajevo, Yugoslavia. . First Eastern European country to hold the Games.

1988 Calgary, Canada.

1992 Albertville, France.

Giant and supergiant slalom

There are three types of slalom event in competition skiing: giant slalom, supergiant slalom and slalom. You can find out about these over the next four pages.

Giant slalom

Giant slalom combines some of the speed and excitement of downhill racing while also demanding nimble, fast turns. It is considered by experts to be the most physically, technically and athletically demanding alpine event.

The timing begins when the skier passes through the starting gate.

Starting order

The starting order in the first run is worked out according to the number of points competitors have accumulated in previous F.I.S. events. The highest ranked skiers go first.

In the second run, the five fastest competitors in the first run go first in reverse order - the fifth-fastest first, then the fourth-fastest - and so on. The fastest skier in the first run has the advantage of knowing what times to beat.

The starting order for giant slalom is also the same for the other slalom events.

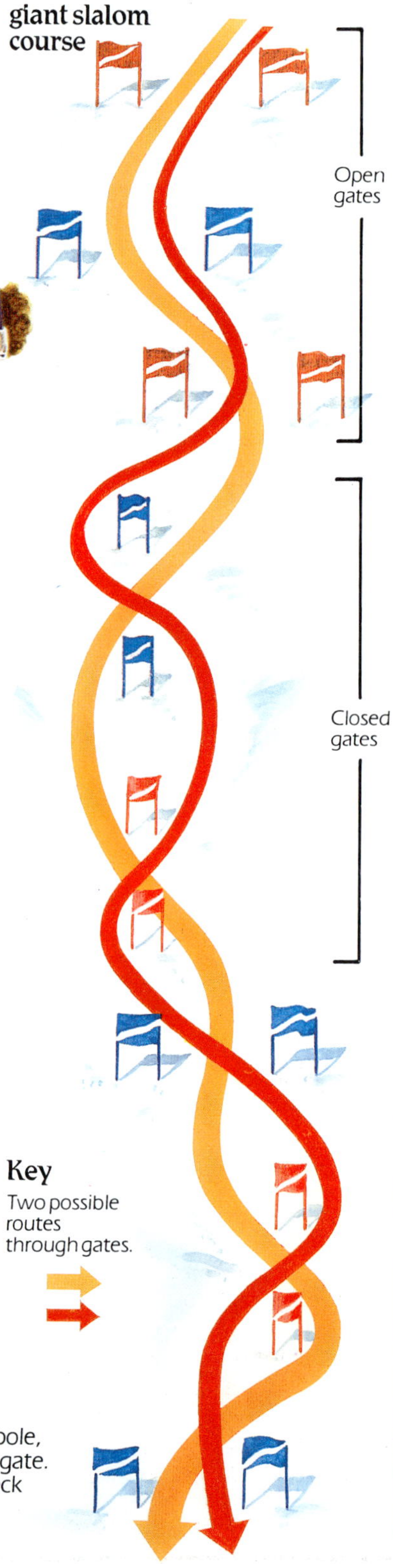

The skier is allowed to knock a gate pole, but both skis must pass through the gate. There are judges by each gate to check that they do.

The course

The course is laid out to allow the competitor to ski it in a flowing manner whilst at the same time testing a variety of techniques.

There are strict F.I.S. rules governing course preparation. Excessively sharp ridges, ledges that would cause the skier to leave the ground for long distances and hidden obstacles, must be removed. There must be enough turning gates to limit the skier to a safe speed. The snow must be as hard as possible and if snow falls during the race, it must be removed or compacted.

Each course must have a drop of 250-400 metres in men's events, 250-350 metres in women's events, with a minimum drop of 300 metres for both sexes in World Cup events. The course should also be hilly.

The number of gates in each course must be within 12-15% of the vertical drop in metres. For example, a course with a 400 metre drop must have 48 to 60 gates. There should be both single gates and chicanes of multiple gates.

The most direct line down a slope is called the fall line.

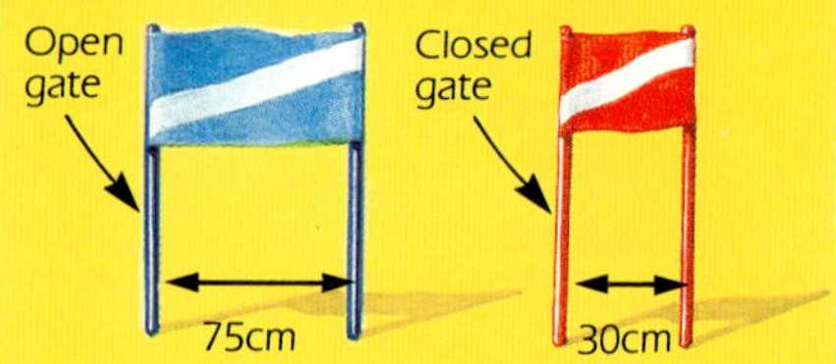

The gates can be "open" - that is, positioned horizontally across the fall line - or "closed" - that is lying along the fall line (see left). They must be 4-8m wide with a minimum distance between them of 10m.

Each gate consists of two pairs of poles, each pair linked to a banner. The poles for closed gates are 30cm apart and 75cm apart for open gates.

The race

Before the race, competitors slide alongside the course to study it, but they are not allowed to ski the course itself. The course is then skied by non-competing "forerunners" who mark the path through the gates.

Competitors are judged on two electronically timed runs, done on different courses. Times for both runs are added, and the winner is the one with the shortest overall time.

Giant slalom technique

The skier has to select and follow the best line through the gates, minimize the amount of braking on each turn and accelerate as much as possible between turns.

Because of the high speed of giant slalom, skiers maintain a low stance most of the time and make gentle, rounded turns by steering with their legs and rarely using their poles.

Disqualification

Competitors are disqualified if they receive assistance on the course or do not pass through a gate properly. They can finish on one ski if the other is lost. If disqualified, a competitor cannot continue or go into the second run.

Supergiant slalom

Supergiant slalom, or Super-G, first appeared in the World Cup, amid controversy, in the 1982/3 season. It was intended to be an event even closer to downhill (see page 10) than giant slalom. The course is steeper and has more widely spaced gates than giant slalom, making it a much faster race.

Some people were worried that its inclusion in World Cup events would make the competitors even more specialized, but others looked forward to seeing competitors win prizes in both Super-G and downhill racing.

The course

Skiers compete over one course only. The drop is much greater than in a giant slalom course: 500-600 metres for men and 350-500 metres for women. The maximum number of gates is 10% of the drop (in metres), with a minimum of 35 in men's events and 30 in women's events.

In men's events, two jumps are permitted, one requiring a change of direction and one not. These are provided to add to the interest of the run.

Special equipment

To save vital hundredths of a second, competitors wear low-drag, one-piece clothing. The rules require them to wear crash helmets. Their skis are similar to those used in downhill events (see page 11).

Slalom and parallel slalom

In slalom events, the skier turns continuously down the course through a sequence of gates. It is a test of the skier's technical ability in performing precise, controlled, nimble turns. Speed is also important, but the turns restrict skiers to a maximum of 40km/h.

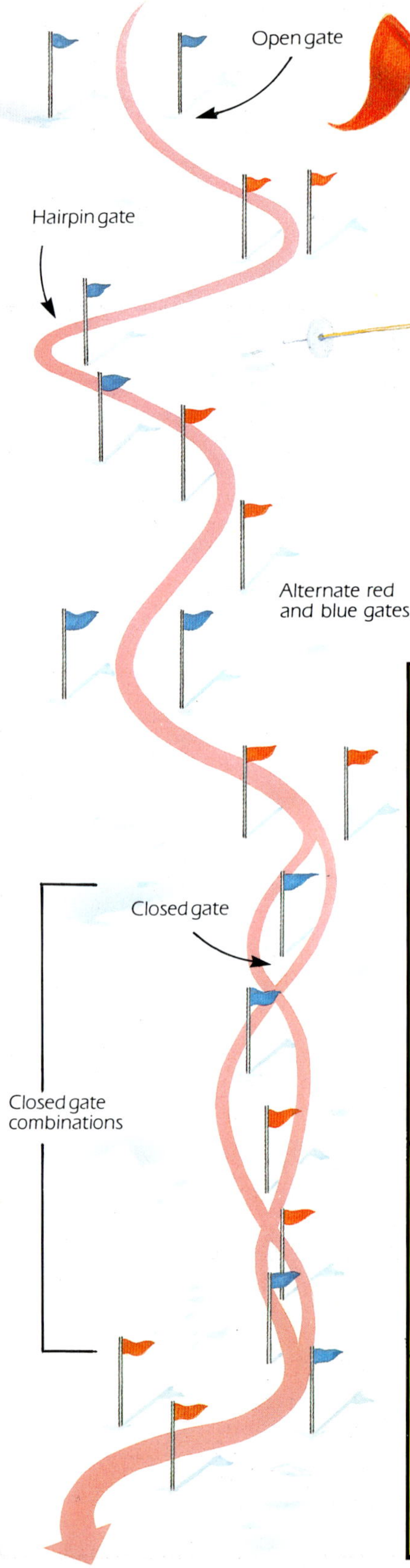

Slalom course

In the Olympic and World Championship events, a slalom course should have a drop of 180-220 metres for men and 130-180 metres for women. At other international events, the drop need only be 140-220 metres and 120-180 metres respectively.

In World Championship and Olympic events the angle of the slope is also specified. It should be between 18 and 24 degrees and, for very short stretches, as much as 27 degrees.

Within these limits, there is a wide freedom of choice in laying out the gates. The aim is to create a run which gives competitors the opportunity to combine maximum speed with maximum skill and elegance in the turns. There must be a combination of single and multiple gates, some traverses and plenty of tight turns. There should be a minimum of four hairpin gates and two combinations of closed gates, as shown on the right.

The difficulty of the course is geared to the average ability of the best 30 competitors.

The snow on the course must be even harder than in the other slalom events.

Slalom gates

The sides of slalom gates are marked by single poles carrying a flag. The gates are smaller and closer together than in giant slalom. Each gate is 4-6 metres wide. The distance between open gates is 7-15 metres and not less than 0.75 metres between closed gates. There are 55-75 gates in men's events and 45-60 gates in women's events, depending on the length of the course.

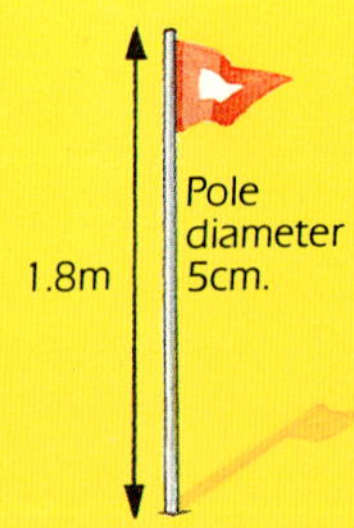

A competitor who knocks over a pole on a turn will not be disqualified even if it comes out of the snow, as long as both skis pass through the gate.

Slalom skiers maintain a much higher body position than in giant slalom as the emphasis is on rapid turns rather than increasing speed between turns.

Slalom techniques

Slalom skiers aim to choose the "best" line through the gates, which is not necessarily the shortest route. "Good" and "bad" lines are shown on the right. The skiers aim to turn before the gate rather than after it so that they do not have to brake sharply and can make smooth, rounded turns. These are faster than short, skidded turns.

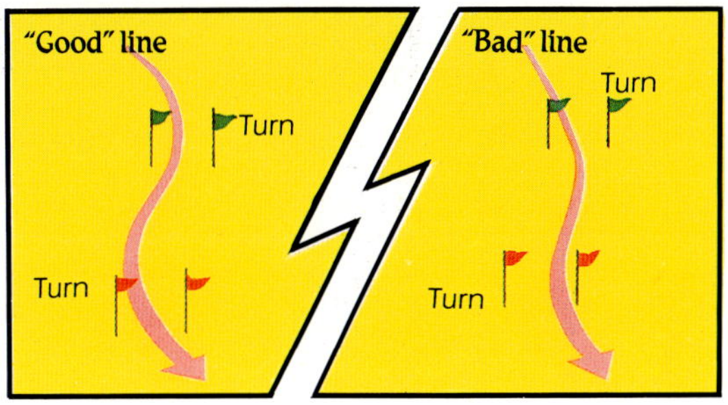

The techniques used by slalom skiers varies. Some experts succeed by taking a "bad line" because they are so fast on the turns.

Parallel slalom

In parallel slalom competitors race each other rather than the clock down identical courses. Each contest is based on two runs. Skiers swap courses for the second run. Electronic timing records the difference between the finishing times of the competitors in thousandths of a second. The winner is decided on the combined time differences of the two runs.

The competition is organized on a knockout basis, with five rounds. The winner of each goes through to the next round, as shown below. The overall winner skis 10 races in succession.

This event has not yet been accepted in the Olympics and is only occasionally allowed to contribute to World Cup points. It is very exciting to watch, so is a popular event.

The course

The twin courses must be as nearly identical as possible. They are much shorter than for the single slalom event, with a drop of 80-100 metres and 20-30 gates. The race only lasts for about 20 to 25 seconds.

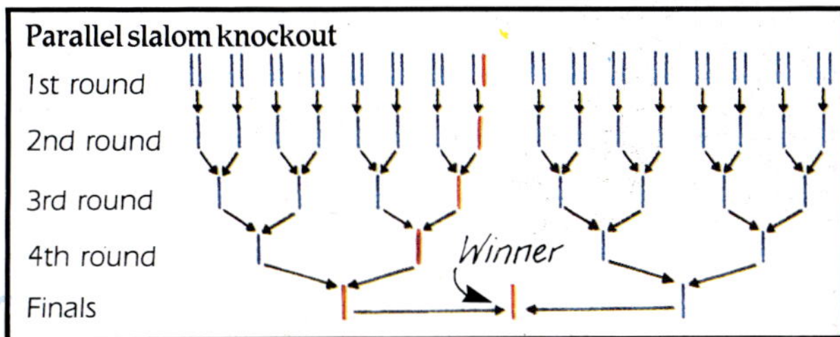

The race

The starting gates lift automatically when the starting gun is fired. A fast start is important, as the skier who is first away is often the first to finish.

If both competitors fall, the one who goes over the finish line first, wearing both skis, wins.

If one competitor fails to finish, he or she is disqualified. If both fail to finish, the one who skied furthest down the course goes through to the next round.

Digital clock

The slalom race

The winner is the skier with the fastest combined time over two runs done on different courses. Competitors are timed electronically, as in other alpine events.

The starting order is decided in the same way as for giant slalom (see page 6).

The gate poles are the same as for giant slalom.

Downhill and the flying kilometre

Downhill racing is the oldest and most spectacular alpine skiing event. Competitors ski as fast as 140km/h, in a race against the clock on courses groomed to make them as safe as possible.

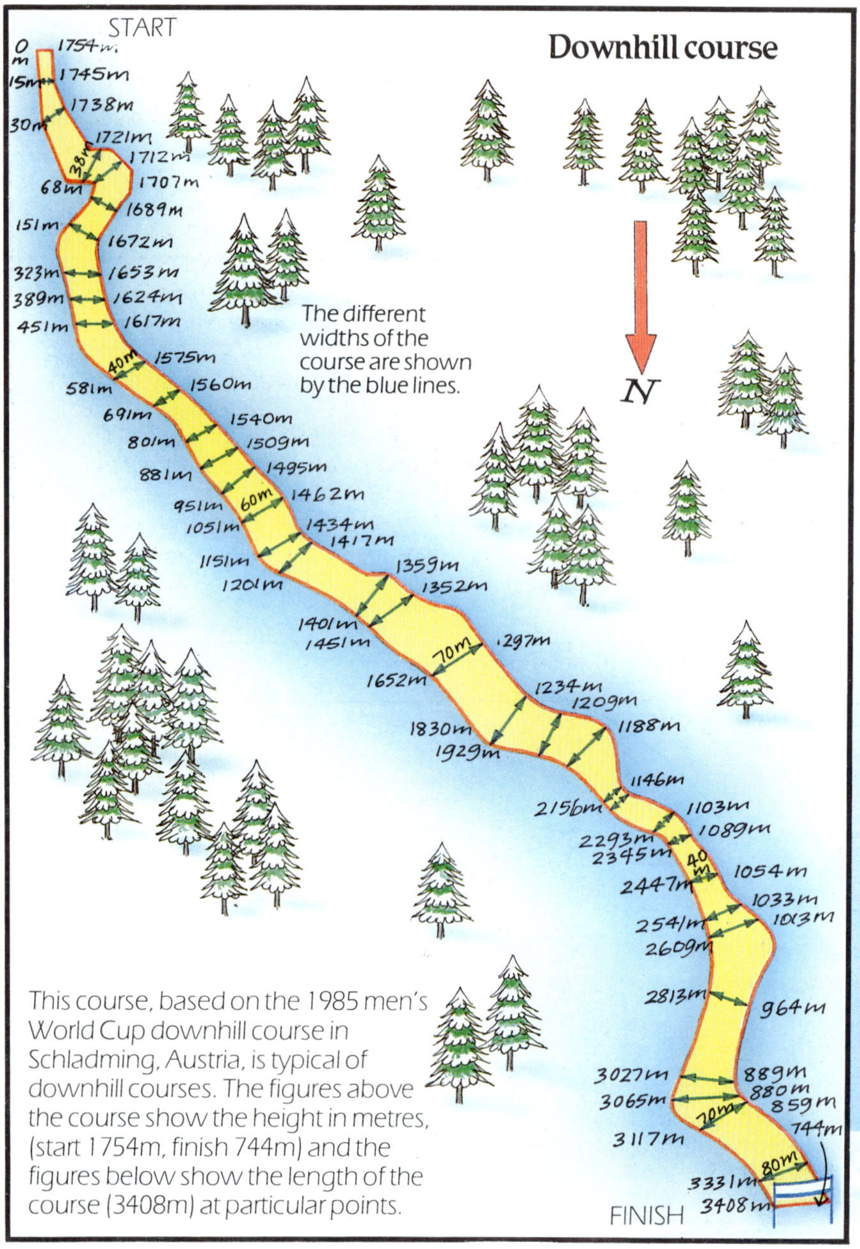

This course, based on the 1985 men's World Cup downhill course in Schladming, Austria, is typical of downhill courses. The figures above the course show the height in metres, (start 1754m, finish 744m) and the figures below show the length of the course (3408m) at particular points.

The course

In major downhill events, the drop is 800-1000 metres for men and 500-700 metres for women. The competition is judged on one run only, but can be split into two runs of at least 450 metres each if the necessary drop cannot be achieved in one course. This is not allowed in the World and Continental Cups.

The course must be smooth and steep enough for skiers to schuss (ski straight down) all the way without needing to use their poles.

F.I.S. regulations state that it must not be possible to complete a men's course in less than 2 minutes or a women's course in less than 1 minute 40 seconds. All obstacles, bumps and hard ridges are removed and gates are placed along the course to limit the skier's speed.

For safety reasons, the course must be at least 30 metres wide where it is bordered by trees. Where the course bends, there must be clear areas each side to limit the risk of injury if a skier goes off the course.

Twigs and pine needles are strewn on the course to help the skiers see bumps and dips. This is particularly important in poor visibility.

Training for the race

All competitors must complete strictly controlled, compulsory training on the course before the event. This takes place over three days, although in very bad weather, the time is reduced. There have to be at least three training runs and competitors are timed on at least one of them.

Starting order

The top fifteen skiers from previous results start first. Their starting order is determined by a draw. The other competitors start in order of their previous results. The first fifteen have an advantage over the others, as the course is usually at its best before too many competitors have skied it.

Downhill technique

Speed is the most important factor in ▶ downhill racing so competitors must keep their wind resistance as low as possible. This is done by adopting the "egg position" between turns, as shown to the right.

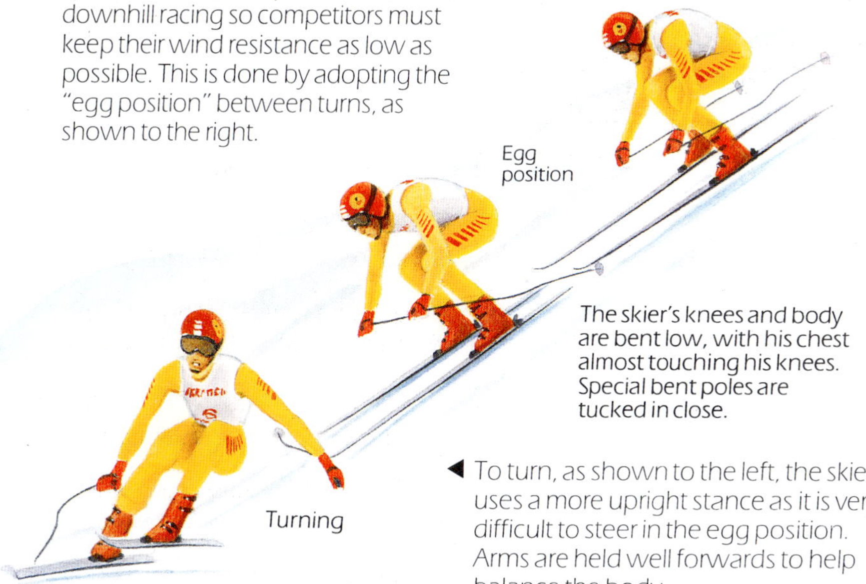

The skier's knees and body are bent low, with his chest almost touching his knees. Special bent poles are tucked in close.

◀ To turn, as shown to the left, the skier uses a more upright stance as it is very difficult to steer in the egg position. Arms are held well forwards to help balance the body.

Throughout the course, the skiers absorb bumps with their knees while keeping the pressure of the skis constant on the snow. Some bumps make skiers take off and lose contact with the snow. This slows them down. To compensate, skiers often "pre-jump" before a bump to help stay on the snow, as shown below. ▼

Pre-jumping

Downhill courses also include larger jumps. Competitors keep as low as possible as they take off, to lessen their wind resistance.

Equipment

Downhill skis are long, about 215-230cm, fairly wide and heavy. The poles are bent so that they fit around the body to help lessen wind resistance.

All racers wear one-piece lightweight suits, designed to keep down wind resistance. Crash helmets are compulsory.

The flying kilometre

The flying kilometre is a speed trial, restricted by F.I.S. regulations to men only. In a straight downhill schuss, competitors reach speeds of over 200 km/h. This is not an Olympic event, nor an official part of the skiing calendar, but there are usually 3-5 contests per year.

The course is perfectly smooth, with no turns or obstacles. After a run-in, the slope gradually increases to 45°. The skier is electronically timed over the last 100 metres of this slope.

At the end of the course, the slope gradually flattens and then goes slightly uphill over at least 300 metres. The run-out at the end of the course is often the most dangerous part, as the skier's body can be flung off balance as his skis slow down.

Speed equipment

Specialized aerodynamic equipment is extremely important in order to break speed records. Competitors use long skis, tight-fitting boots, aerodynamically designed crash helmets and skin-tight suits. Poles are bent, as for downhill racing.

Ski jumping

Ski jumping was originated by Sondre Norheim in Norway about 100 years ago, and is one of the oldest competitive skiing events. Ski jumping is highly specialized and is restricted to men only. For most skiers, it is only a spectator sport. Skiers launch themselves into the air at about 100 km/h from specially built jumps – the aim being to stay in the air for as long as possible, whilst maintaining perfect control and style.

Ski jumping is held as an individual event and together with the 15 kilometre cross-country race in the Nordic combined event (see page 14).

Before the competition begins, trial jumps are made by non-competitors. These jumps, together with snow conditions and wind speed, determine how long the in-run should be so that the jumpers land on or around the table-point.

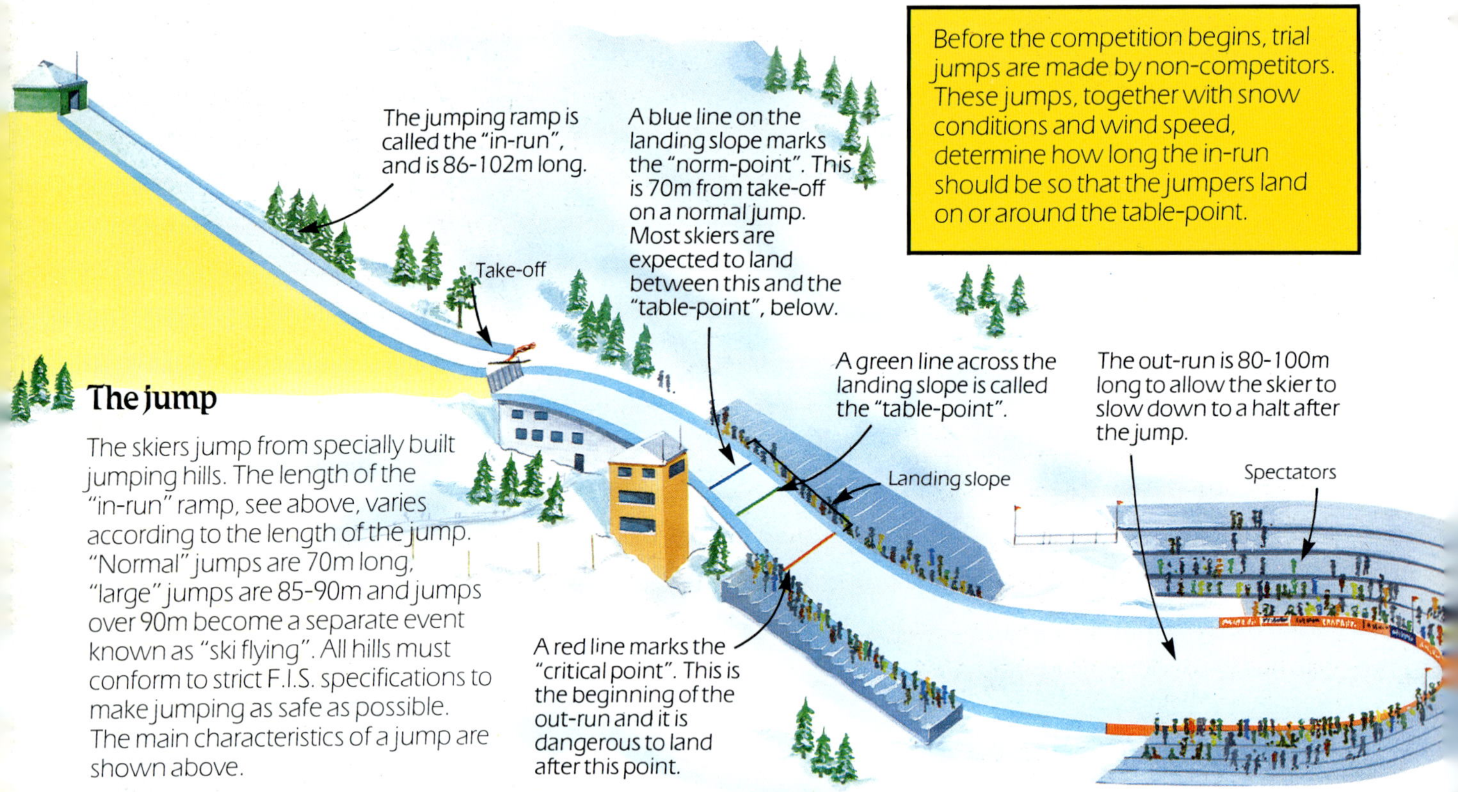

The jump

The skiers jump from specially built jumping hills. The length of the "in-run" ramp, see above, varies according to the length of the jump. "Normal" jumps are 70m long, "large" jumps are 85-90m and jumps over 90m become a separate event known as "ski flying". All hills must conform to strict F.I.S. specifications to make jumping as safe as possible. The main characteristics of a jump are shown above.

Ski jumping technique

The skier skis down the in-run to the take-off in the "egg position", picking up as much speed as possible. No ski poles are allowed, and the skier holds his hands behind his body.

On take-off, the skier will reach speeds of up to 105 km/h. He jumps by stretching his legs sharply and pushing off with his feet to propel his body upwards and forwards over the ski tips.

In the air, his skis are parallel and fairly close. He leans over his skis and keeps his arms close to his body. To begin with, the ski tips tilt up slightly to give aerodynamic lift, like an aircraft wing.

What the judges look for

Each competitor is judged on two jumps, although they can do an optional trial jump first. The scores for the two jumps are added for the final result.

In a perfect jump, the skier keeps his skis close together, parallel and horizontal. He must not wave his arms in flight, although he can use his arms to maintain balance when landing. The F.I.S. regulations state that: "The ideal jump shall be executed with power, boldness and precision. It shall at the same time give the impression of calmness, steadiness and control".

Ski-jumping style has changed over the years. This picture shows what was considered to be "perfect style" in the 1930s, which is very different to the aerodynamic positions used by ski-jumpers today.

Scoring

Scores are awarded for style and the length of the jump, measured from take-off to landing.

Points for the length of the jump are taken from the distance beyond the norm-point.

There are five style judges. The skier begins with 20 points, losing them for faults. Faults in the in-run and out-run are not counted, although the take-off, flight and landing must be perfect for maximum points. If the skier falls or touches the snow with his hands after landing, he receives an automatic penalty of 10 points. The highest and lowest of the five style scores are discarded, so just three scores count.

Special equipment

Ski jumpers wear one-piece, lightweight, close-fitting clothing to keep the wind resistance as low as possible. The skis are much longer, wider, heavier and have more grooves underneath than normal cross-country skis, to help give lift and stability in flight. Special bindings allow the jumper to lean right forward. Helmets are worn for safety reasons.

The skier remains in the aerodynamic position until just before landing. To prepare for landing, the skier stretches his legs beneath him and stretches out his arms. He moves one ski in front of the other (into the telemark position), and bends his knees to absorb the shock as he lands.

The flight position reduces wind resistance as much as possible. In this position, the skier can take corrective action if he is hit by a gust of wind - one of the main dangers in ski jumping.

Cross-country racing and biathlon

The first skiing competitions were races on cross-country skis. Today, cross-country racing is split into five main events: individual racing, relay racing, the Nordic combined (jumping and racing), the biathlon (shooting and racing combined), and marathons.

All these events are held in varied, rolling countryside, with a mixture of downhill, uphill and flat sections. There are rules about the amount and length of climbs on each course. The skiers ski in tracks, or skate on a pisted way with refreshment stations every 7-8km.

Individual racing

Competitors in this event leave the starting line at 30 second intervals for a race against the clock. The skier with the fastest time wins.

In the Olympics and World Cup, the courses are 10-50km for men, and 5-20km for women.

Techniques used

Traditional cross-country includes the diagonal stride, double pole-push, herringbone and downhill techniques. In the early 1980's traditionalists were upset by the use of the skating step (pushing with the ski at an angle to the track). It is faster than older techniques but lacks grace and destroys the tracks.

After much debate, the F.I.S. ruled that the skating step can be used in half of the 1986/7 and 1987/8 World Cup events, and in the 1988 Olympics. Traditional events will be called "classic", and others which include skating steps will be called "freestyle" events. The future of classic and freestyle techniques depends on how popular they are over the next few seasons.

Overtaking

Skiers must give way to let faster skiers overtake.

Relay

Relay racing rules are the same as for individual racing, but with a few additions. The skiers compete in teams of four and each person skis on one leg of the course. There are four 10km legs in men's events and four 5km legs in women's events.

The first skiers in each team start together. After the first 100 metres, the starting tracks converge to form three tracks. At the end of each leg there is a 30m change over area where the skiers hand-over by touching the next skier in their team.

Equipment

Cross-country racers use skis specialized for either the classic-style or the skating step. Classic skiers may occasionally need to stop and rewax their skis on long races. Competitors may replace both poles during the race, but only one ski, making the change without assistance. They wear lightweight, one-piece clothing.

Nordic combined

The Nordic combined is regarded by many as the elite Nordic event, but it is still confined to men only. The competition takes place over three days. Normally on the first two days each competitor does three jumps from a 70km hill, of which the best two count. On the third day they enter a 15km cross-country race. The winner is determined by the combined results.

Biathlon

The biathlon combines cross-country racing with target shooting, having its origins in the use of skis for military purposes and hunting. Most competitors in this specialized event train in their armed forces. This is the only event not governed by the F.I.S., but by a body called the Union International de Pentathlon Moderne et Biathlon.

There are three main events in the World Cup and Olympics, outlined below.

20km race

The course has five 4km cross-country loops which are arranged around a central point where the starting line, finishing line and rifle ranges are set. The course itself must have height differences of 550-750m.

The skiers carry 4.5kg rifles on their back and 20 rounds of ammunition. At the end of all except the last loop, the skiers enter the firing range and fire five rounds at targets 50m away. A one minute penalty is added to a competitor's overall time for each target left standing. An average time for completing such a course is one hour.

Equipment

The rifles must not have a telescopic sight. Clothing is light-weight, but is often strengthened at the elbows and on one shoulder for firing lying down. One ski can be replaced if necessary during the race, and a spare rifle can be kept at the range.

10km sprint

The 10km sprint is divided into three loops with a height distance over the course of 300-400m. There are two firing sessions, one lying down and the other standing. In this event, for each target missed the competitor skis a penalty loop of 150 metres, which takes about 30 seconds to do.

30km relay

There are four biathletes in each relay team. Each member skis 7.5km with two firing sessions, one lying down and the other standing. As with cross-country relay, there is a mass start by all the first skiers.

Marathons

Ski marathons, called "citizen racing" in America, are long distance races (from 40-150km) which anyone can enter. They are very popular and can attract mass starts of over 10,000 skiers of all ages and abilities, showing that cross-country racing is an Olympic sport that is also widely practised by ordinary people.

Some marathons, such as the Canadian ski marathon, are two day events in which advanced competitors camp out overnight.

Ten of the world's major marathons have grouped together to form Worldloppet, an international ski series. Anyone who competes in all of them in the course of their life receives a special medal.

Aerials and moguls

There are three kinds of freestyle skiing, called aerials, mogul skiing and ballet. Aerials and mogul skiing are explained here; freestyle ballet and its techniques on pages 18-19.

History of freestyle

Freestyle is new to competitive skiing, and will be introduced as a demonstration sport for the first time at the 1988 Olympic Games in Calgary, Canada.

Freestyle developed in America in the late sixties/seventies as an attempt to break away from strictly stylized skiing, such as "perfect" parallel turns, and to add more freedom, fun and challenge to skiing. Most skiing competitions began on an amateur basis, but freestyle competition started as a professional sport. The attraction of prize money and the lack of set rules, led competitors to take many risks. In 1973, following some serious accidents, the freestyle skiers organized themselves into a professional body to control safety and draw up competition rules. In 1979, freestyle was accepted into the F.I.S., the organization which governs all skiing competitions, and freestyle gained the credibility it had previously lacked.

Aerials

Aerials are the most exciting of the three freestyle disciplines. They can also be very dangerous, and the rules drawn up by the F.I.S. are particularly strict.

The three main types of aerial manoeuvres are jumps called uprights, front somersaults and back somersaults. The easiest jumps are uprights, such as the side twist. The helicopter is also an upright jump but it is slightly more complicated as it involves a 360° spin.

Side twist

Helicopter

Somersault

Somersaults are the most difficult and spectacular aerials. The photographs above show a layout back somersault.

Safety

No jumps should be attempted without qualified instruction. Training begins on trampolines which help to increase body awareness in flight. The pupil then practises on artificial jumps into water. Once the aerial manoeuvre and landing has been perfected in this way, the pupil can attempt aerials on snow. All aerial competitors need to present a certificate of competence from a qualified judge or an experienced jumper.

Take off

In all aerial competitions, the skier takes off from a specially built jump, called a kicker. There are usually three different heights of kickers depending on whether a single, double or triple somersault is being performed. The highest, most steeply curved kicker is used for triple somersaults. Upright jumps, as well as single somersaults, are performed from the smallest kicker.

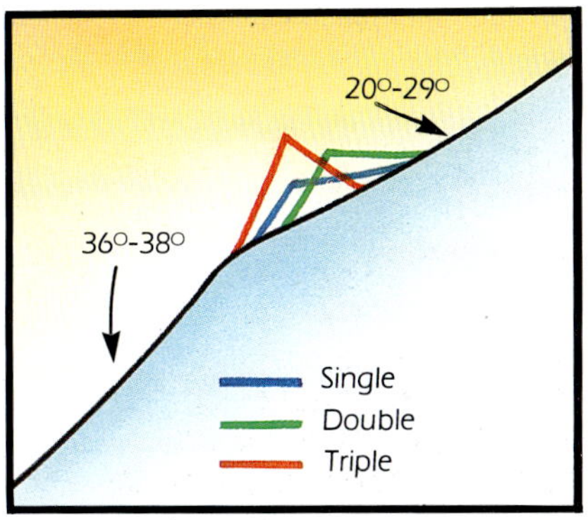

The run in slope to the kickers is at an angle of 20° to 29°. The landing slope needs to be within the angles of 36° to 38° to prevent hard impact on landing. The landing slope itself is continually softened with a shovel to ease landing.

What the judges look for

In the past, jumps were judged according to how visually exciting they were. Now, in the interest of safety, the emphasis is on perfection. Before each jump, the competitor informs the jury of the figure he is to perform.

Scores are awarded in the following manner:

* Technical performance (out of 5)
* Height and distance (out of 2)
* Extent of jump & landing (out of 3)

Complex jumps performed well are worth more than simple jumps. The judges multiply the score for each jump by a factor based on the degree of difficulty of the jump to reach a final score.

Mogul skiing

Moguls are bumps on a steep slope, made by many skiers turning in the same places. Their skis dig out ruts and spray the snow into bumps.

In mogul skiing, competitors ski a mogul slope to loud music, jumping and turning very often, using upright aerials only.

A course is about 250m long, with a 28°-35° incline. Skiers start through a gate which triggers the electronic timing.

There is a smooth, clear area at the bottom of the course where skiers come to a controlled stop. The judges stand below this, where they can see the whole slope.

Jumps, such as the "mule kick" above, are scored highly in mogul skiing. Landing is difficult on a steep mogul slope, and the skier must time the jump perfectly in order not to break the continuity of the run. The skier wears bright knee pads to heighten his movements.

What the judges look for

Scores are awarded in the following manner:

* Technique, i.e. ease of action on a very uneven course (out of 5)
* The two best jumps (out of 2.5)
* Electronically timed speed (out of 2.5).

At the beginning of the competition, a finalist from a previous competition skis the course and acts as a pace setter for speed. The speed points for each competitor are set against this.

The top 8 go through to the finals, which are held in pairs - two finalists compete side by side down the course.

Ballet and simple ballet technique

Freestyle ballet is a mixture of figure skating and gymnastics performed on snow. The skier "dances" to music broadcast over a smooth 250m course, sloping at 11° to 16°. The snow should be dry, well packed and easy to ski on.

Ballet technique

Freestyle ballet can be done by any competent skier. The only limits are your level of fitness and imagination. For ballet skiing you need a good sense of balance and the ability to shift your weight freely from one ski to another. The techniques shown here will help you develop these skills and improve your normal alpine skiing, as well as giving you the freedom and fun of trying something new.

Royal Christie

The Royal Christie is said to be named after a German ice skater, Fritz Reuel (pronounced royal), who wrote the first book on ballet skiing in 1929*. A Royal Christie is a turn made on the inside ski with the outside ski raised backwards as high as possible.

Begin in the traverse position with your weight on the lower ski.

Plant your inside pole and start lifting the upper ski slightly to the side and behind.

Uphill crossover

The uphill crossover is also known as a stepover. You need to be supple for this manoeuvre, so make sure you do not try it until you are thoroughly warmed up. You can do exercises to help warm your legs up and strengthen the muscles.

Start by skiing across the fall line with your right leg back and to the side.

Rock your right ski back and then kick it high up in front of you, crossing it over the left ski.

360° spin

The 360° spin is a basic manoeuvre used a lot in freestyle ballet. Once you have mastered the basic spin shown to the right, with practice you will be able to spin round two or three times in the same way.

Start by skiing across the hill with your arms out to your sides in a ballet position.

Plant your upper pole, and bend your knees up into the hill to begin the turn.

Judging

Scores are awarded out of 10 like this:

* Choreography (the ballet sequence) and originality (out of 2.5)
* Difficulty of the manoeuvres (out of 2.5)
* Technical achievement and overall impression (out of 5)

Technical achievement points are given for the degree of perfection of the figures, independently of how difficult they are.

Fritz Reuel: New Possibilities in Skiing.

The outrigger

The outrigger is a simple freestyle manoeuvre which can be used to link up more difficult manoeuvres or when coming out of a turn. It is basically a traverse done in a low position, with the lower leg stretched out below the upper leg, as shown to the right.

Begin by traversing across the hill.

Bend down and stretch your lower ski out to the side.

Continue traversing in this low position.

Bend forward at the waist and arch your back. Begin turning by shifting weight onto the front of the ski.

With your ski flat on the snow, lean your head and shoulders into the turn. The ski will follow round.

Decrease the pressure on the front of the ski, so that the tail of the ski slips down.

Bring the lifted ski down next to the new upper ski, and return to the traverse position.

Put your right ski down about 30cm from the left ski, and shift your weight onto it.

Using your poles for balance, bend forwards at your waist and lift your left ski up behind you.

Straighten up your body and bring the left ski round parallel to the right ski.

Complete the crossover by putting down the left ski, and ski on in a ballet stance.

You will now be half way through the spin, facing directly up the hill. Keep your weight forwards.

Lean back onto the tails of your skis so that the tips swing round for the second half of the spin.

With your weight on the front of your skis push your knees forwards into the rest of the spin.

The 360° spin is now complete and you should be facing in the same direction as you started.

Ice-skating events

Ice skating events offer a wide variety of sport – high-speed racing in speed skating, technique and artistic interpretation in figure skating and team skill in ice-hockey. All the events on these pages are in the Olympics, except short track speed skating, which is a demonstration event at Calgary in 1988.

Ice-hockey

Ice-hockey is a fast team game, played on a marked sheet of ice 56m by 26m, enclosed by boards 115cm high. You can see the markings below. Teams have up to twenty players, though only six are on the ice at one time (three attack and three defence players). The rest sit on the bench until sent on by their coach as substitutes, which happens all the time as the game is very tiring.

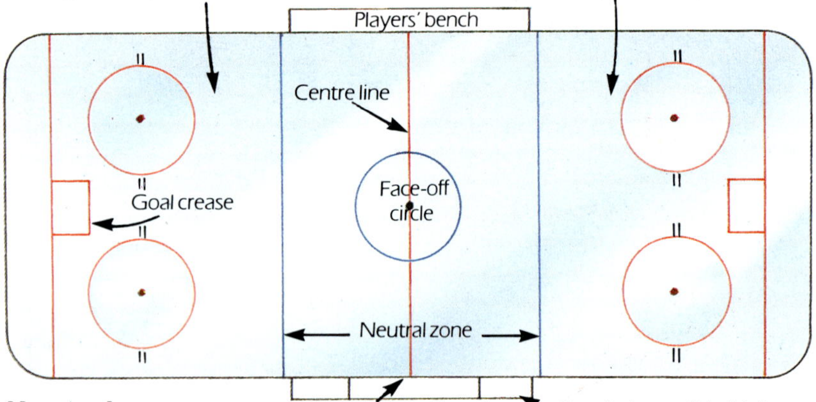

How to play

Teams try to score goals by hitting the puck (see below) into the other team's goal net. There are three twenty-minute periods. To start each one there is a face-off. The referee drops the puck between two opposing players, who fight for possession of it with their sticks. The winner and his team pass the puck to one another along the ice and try to hit it into their opponents' goal. Opposing team members tackle players or intercept passes to try and get the puck. Breaking rules results in a penalty time of between two and fifteen minutes spent in the penalty box, or sin-bin. If the penalty is for ten minutes or less, the player may not be substituted and his team must play with one man missing. Up to two players who help set up a goal are credited with an "assist".

The equipment

The goaltender on the left shows the kind of protective gear players wear. International standards for the gear are always being improved. Sticks are light and made mostly of wood. The puck is a hard rubber disc, 7.6cm across and 2.5cm deep. The goal is 1.22m high, 1.83m wide and is not fixed, so it moves if crashed into.

Figure skating

Figure skating consists of men's and ladies' individual events, pair skating and ice dance. In each event there are different sections to test technique and inventiveness (see right).

Skates

To understand figure skating, it helps to know about the skates and their specialized blades, since scoring points depends on the correct use of them.

The boots are laced quite tightly to above the ankle to give support. The blade is curved from front to back and has two edges with a hollow between (see below).

The jagged points on the front of the blade are called toe rakes or picks. They are used to help the skater launch high into the air for jumps.

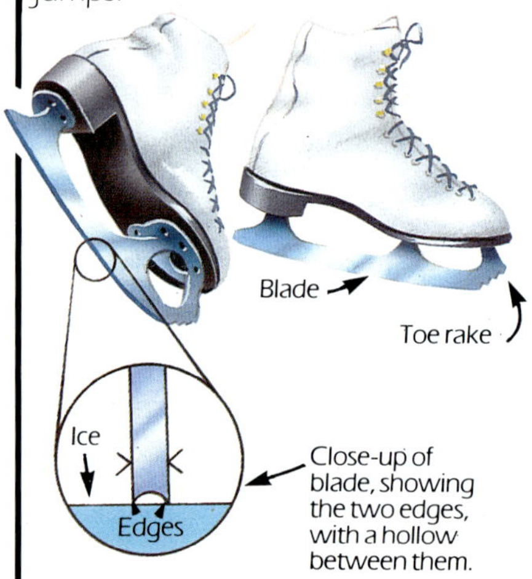

On either skate, the edge that is nearest the other foot is called the inside edge and the edge furthest from the other foot is called the outside edge.

Scoring in figure skating

Most events have seven or nine judges. In each section, each judge gives every competitor a mark out of six. Added together, these give the competitor's placing in that section – highest score gets first place, second-highest second place and so on.

The events

Here are the main events in figure skating, and the sections within them. All of them are Olympic events.

Event	Sections
Men's and women's individual	Compulsory Short Programme Free skating
Pairs	Short programme Free skating
Ice dance	Compulsory Original Set Pattern Free dance

Compulsory. Specific figures (patterns on the ice, such as a figure eight) or dance movements are performed as technically perfectly as possible. Each part of a figure must be done on a specified edge of the blade (see left). Putting both edges on the ice at the same time is called a "flat" and is a serious mistake.

Short programme. Skaters must do seven set elements within a time limit. They can do them in any order, to music of their choice. They must repeat the sequence three times, identically.

This pair is performing a figure called a death spiral.

Original set pattern (OSP). The skaters devise their own routine to a specified dance rhythm, such as a waltz or quickstep. The routine must cover the whole area of the ice and be repeated identically three times.

Free skating. A number of jumps, turns and linking steps have to be included, but skaters are free to choose exactly which ones. They perform to music of their choice and are judged on artistic impression and the harmony of the routine as well as technical mastery.

Placings are then multiplied by a different factor for each section to give penalty points. These are added together to give a final result. In ice dance, for example, the placings are multiplied by 0.6 for Compulsory, 0.4 for Original Set Pattern and 1.0 for Free skating. A pair placed second, say, in each section must multiply each of the factors by two. The skater with the fewest penalty points wins. In a draw, the highest scorer in the Free skating wins.

Speed skating

Speed skating consists of timed racing events over several fixed distances, which differ for men and women (see below).

Skating style

Speed skaters adopt a low, leaning-forward position and make long, gliding strokes along the ice. They swing their arms initially to increase their speed, but may then hold them behind their backs, especially in long distance races (3,000, 5,000 and 10,000 metres). This saves energy and makes them streamlined. Their close-fitting clothes help keep wind resistance down.

Speed skates consist of a light shoe, with no ankle support and a long, straight blade. The blade is reinforced to withstand great speed.

This skater shows the typical crouched style speed skaters use.

The track

Speed skating is usually done outdoors, though an indoor track has been built for the Olympics in Calgary. The track is normally a 400m oval divided into two lanes. Two skaters race at a time and swap lanes on each lap to even out the distance skated. Coloured armbands show which lane they started in. Where they swap lanes is called the crossing zone. Competitors are racing against the clock, so the skater with the fastest time wins.

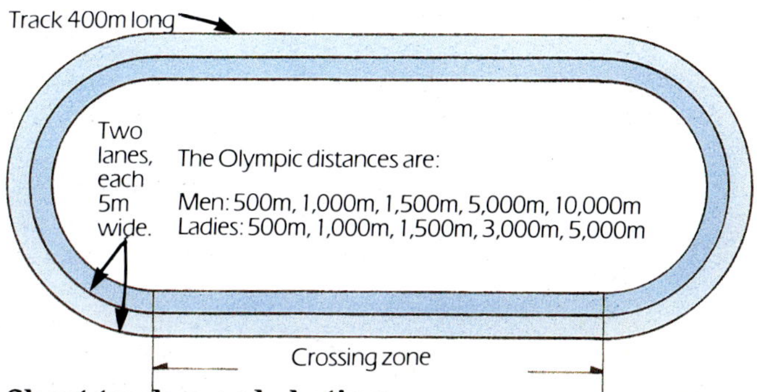

Short track speed skating

Short track speed skating differs from other speed skating events in that it is usually done indoors on tracks with shorter straights and sharper corners. Several skaters race at once and their finishing position, not their time, determines who wins.

Bobsleigh, luge and curling

Bobsleigh and luge are both high-speed sled events down specially prepared courses. Curling is a team sport which is a demonstration event (see page 5) in the Olympic Games at Calgary in 1988. Below, you can find out a bit more about each of these sports.

Bobsleigh

The bobsleigh is a sled with a front that looks a bit like a racing car. Races are restricted to men only at present and World Championships are held every year, except when the Winter Olympics take their place.

About bobsleighs

Bobsleighs (which hold four men) and boblets (the name for the two-man bobsleigh) have four steel runners and a fibreglass cowling, or hood. There are handles on each side for push-starting and they are steered by a rope and toggle system. There is a brake, but it is not used in a descent except in emergencies and at the end of the race. Bobsleighs achieve speeds of up to 150km/h (about 93mph).

Bobsleighs must not exceed the size and weight restrictions given below.

	Two-man	Four-man
Width	86cm	87cm
Length	2.7m	3.8m
Weight of bob + team	390kg	630kg

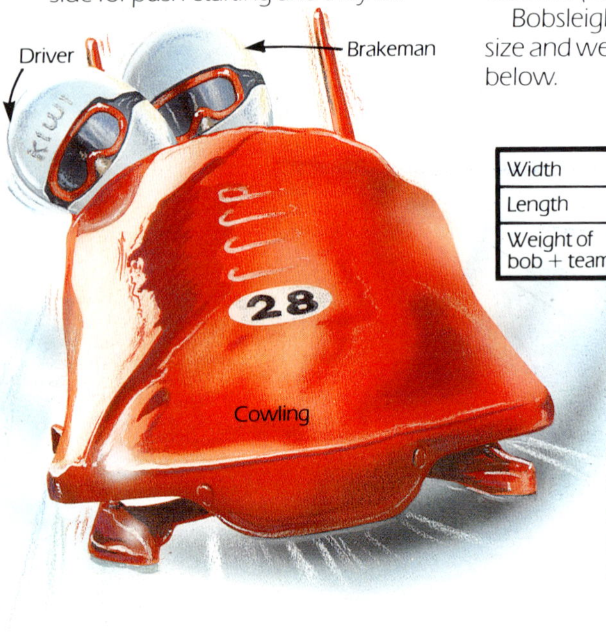

The heavier the bobsleigh, the faster it will go. Teams whose combined weight is less than that allowed may bolt weights to the bobsleigh to help make up the difference.

How bobsleigh competitions work

There are competitions for two-man and four-man teams. They race against the clock down a steep, twisting, man-made course of packed ice, (see right). They use no brakes, except to stop at the bottom.

Before the race there is a practice period and teams must do a certain number of practice runs to qualify.

Teams make four runs, two on two consecutive days and the team that has the fastest combined time wins. Times are recorded electronically to within 1/100th of a second and are double-checked by timekeepers with stopwatches.

In a race, the team sets off from about 15m behind the start line. The men push the bob to get it going well, before jumping into the sled to make the descent.

The man at the front of the bob is the driver, in charge of steering. The man at the back is the brakeman. In the four-man event, the two middle men help push at the start and help manoeuvre during the run by shifting their weight.

Luge

Luge (pronounced looj in English) is the French word for toboggan. Men and women singles and men-only doubles teams ride light toboggans down a steep, twisting track, like the one shown on the right. In the Olympics, singles do four runs, two on two successive days, and doubles do two runs. Fastest combined times decide the winners.

Below you can see the luge used in Olympic events. There are other types of toboggan, such as those used on the Cresta Run, a famous course in St. Moritz, Switzerland. These are ridden headfirst on the stomach. The Cresta Run has been an Olympic event in the past when the Games were held in St. Moritz. It is still a popular race but, since 1964, the luge as described here has been the official Olympic event.

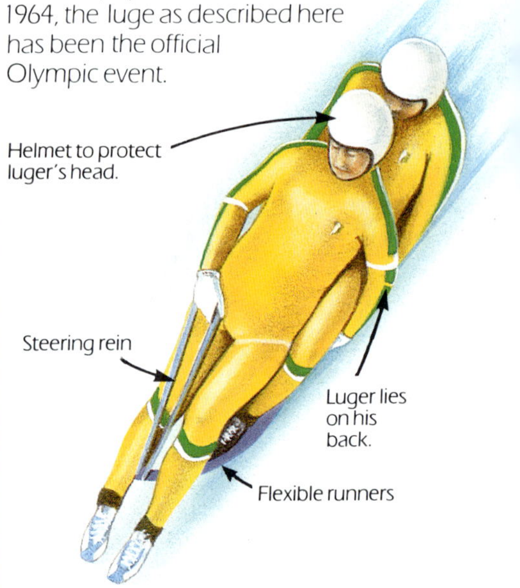

About the luge

A racing luge has two flexible metal runners and a fibreglass seat. Lugers (luge racers) lie on their backs and go down feet first, with their heads slightly raised so they can see where they are going. They steer with reins attached to the runners and by transferring their weight and squeezing the runners with their legs. They reach speeds of up to 125km/h (78mph).

A bobsleigh and luge course

This picture shows the luge and bobsleigh course for the Olympics at Calgary. Beneath it are details of the course.

	Luge Men's	Luge Ladies'	Bob
Start height	1,225m	1,198m	1,241m
Finish height	1,123m	1,123m	1,123m
Drop	104.2m	81.2m	118.2m
Length	1,251m	1,081m	1,474m
Left turns	8	7	8
Right turns	5	3	6
Average gradient	8.3%	7.5%	8%
Max. gradient	19.9%	15%	15%

Making a course

A course is made of stone or concrete with the required gradient and number of curves. It is then covered with hard-packed snow or ice and curves are steeply banked. It may be refrigerated to ensure freezing.

Building a course is very expensive. Some people say it is not worth doing for an Olympics as not enough people use it afterwards. This has been partly overcome by building combined bobsleigh and luge courses so that they can be used for more events.

Curling

In curling, players slide curling stones, or rocks, towards targets on the ice. The sheet of ice is 44.5m long and 4.26m wide with a house (see right), at either end. Teams play from the hacks (rubber grips in the ice) at one end towards the target at the opposite end.

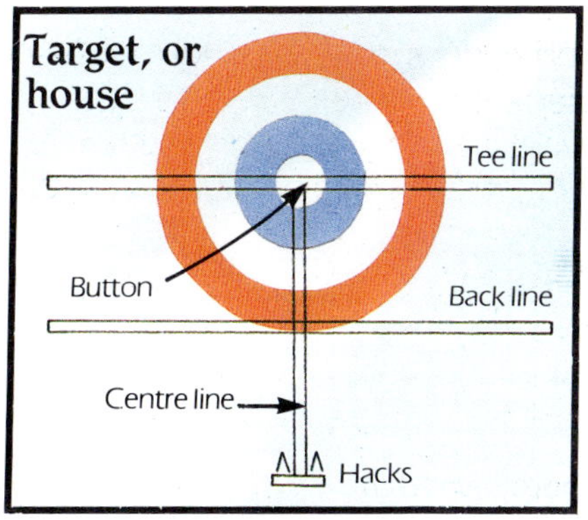

How to play

There are two teams of four players. Each player throws two stones, alternating with one of the other team. First to throw are the "leads." Then come "seconds", "thirds" and "skips" (captains). They all carry brooms. A skip stands on the target and uses his broom to signal what shot to play. The other two team members use theirs to sweep the ice and raise its temperature a fraction, which helps the stone go further.

Curving one stone round another or knocking it out of the way to reach the target are skills of the game.

When all the players have thrown, that completes an "end". Scores are added up and they play in the other direction. Points are scored for each stone that is nearer the centre of the target than any of the other team's. A match either has a number of ends or a time limit.

The curling stone

A curling stone is made of granite. It is circular with a slightly concave top and bottom. It has a smooth surface and a handle which the player twists as he lets go to make it curve across the ice. The band round the middle is called the striking edge. A curling stone can be no more than 91.4cm round and must be not less than 11.4cm high. Maximum weight is 20kg.

Index

First published in 1987 by Usborne Publishing Ltd, 20 Garrick Street, London WC2E 9BJ, England.

Printed in Italy.